THE JOY OF
Hors d'Oeuvre & Cocktails

BEV BENNETT & KIM UPTON

BARRON'S

New York • London • Toronto • Sydney

© Copyright 1984 by Barron's Educational Series

All rights reserved.
No part of this book may be reproduced in any form,
by photostat, microfilm, xerography, or any other
means, or incorporated into any information retrieval
system, electronic or mechanical, without the written
permission of the copyright owner.

All inquiries should be addressed to:

Barron's Educational Series, Inc.
250 Wireless Boulevard
Hauppauge, New York 11788

Cloth Edition
International Standard Book No. 0-8120-5592-6

Paper Edition
International Standard Book No. 0-8120-4280-8

Library of Congress Catalog No. 84-10983

Library of Congress Cataloging in Publication Data

Bennett, Bev.
    The joy of cocktails and hors d' oeurve.
    Includes index.
      1. Cocktails 2. Cookery (Appetizers) I. Upton, Kim.
II Title.
TX951.B415 1984   641.8'12   84-10983
ISBN 0-8120-4280-8 (pbk)
ISBN 0-8120-5592-6

PRINTED AND BOUND IN HONG KONG
901 4900 987654321

Color photography by Matthew Klein
Food stylist, Andrea Swenson
Prop stylist, Linda Cheverton

Accessories courtesy of the following:
China from Villeroy and Boch, Inc.,
41 Madison Avenue, New York City
Crystal and silverware from Royal Copenhagen/
Georg Jenson, 683 Madison Avenue, New York City
Flowers by Ann Titus
Handthrown porcelain from Gordon Foster,
1322 Third Avenue, New York City.

Jacket and cover design by The Sukon Group, Inc.
Book design by Milton Glaser, Inc.